Dearest _____,

Forgiveness

Gateway to Healing

Linda Forster

May God Bless you richly in all things...
Love Sohe

Forgiveness:

Gateway to Healing

Copyright © 2013 by Linda Forster
ISBN:978-1-935765-09-7

Covenant of Peace Ministries
Phone: 717-648-4231
www.covofpeace.org

Scripture quotations are taken from The Amplified Bible, Copyright 1965 by Zondervan Publishing and The New American Standard Bible, Copyright 1971 by The Lockman Foundation

Table of Contents

Chapter One:
Forgiveness, Gateway to Healing.........Page 5

Chapter Two:
Forgiveness Unpacked......................Page 9

Chapter Three:
The Price of Not Forgiving ....Page 17

Chapter Four:
Reconciling Emotional Debt...............Page 41

Chapter Five:
The Process of Forgiving..................Page 49

Chapter One

Forgiveness, Gateway to Healing

"If people truly knew how to forgive, most of the work of modern psychiatry would be unnecessary."
Modern Textbook of Psychiatry

Many have said that forgiveness is the gateway to all healing. In recent years even secular medical and mental health literature acknowledge forgiveness as one of the primary paths to health, both physically and emotionally. Why? Because when we were created, we were neurologically hardwired for relationship. Everything in us desires to be connected to others. When that connection has been broken because of the wounding which occurs between humans, holding on to the offense, hinders one of the very things God placed within us for an abundant life.

Certainly within the Church, forgiveness is founda-

5

tional truth of the Christian faith. However, true, full forgiveness is one of the most misunderstood and misapplied tenets of our faith. We have only to look at Jesus' example on the Cross to understand the truths and depths of forgiveness.

Hanging on the Cross, Jesus suffered in spirit, soul, and body. In His spirit man, He felt the separation from His Father as the sin of the world was put upon Him. Never, up to that point had He felt that isolation, that sense of abandonment, shown by His words, *"Father, Father, why have you forsaken Me?"* Mark 15:34. Jesus also suffered in His soul. He was mocked, spat upon, beaten and ridiculed by the Roman soldiers. Large crowds in Jerusalem for Passover lined the streets at the spectacle of a crucifixion, watching, following and jeering as Jesus struggled to carry the crossbar to Golgotha. Finally, He suffered in His body-- whipped, beaten, and wounded by the crown of thorns--the stress was so great that He sweat drops of blood.

Yet, Jesus' response to the injustice rings down the ages, *"Father, forgive them for they know not what they do."* Luke 23:34. By those words, Jesus demonstrated the reality of healing, of living life with a pure heart, devoted to God, free of offense. Further, in those words, He reflected the love of His Father in manifesting the truth that mercy triumphs over the justice of judgment. His response to the absolute evil that was perpetrated upon Him shows

6

us not only how to be born again through the forgiveness of our sins, but how to live life free of emotional baggage which weighs us down, eventually allowing disease to thrive in our body.

One of God's names is Jehovah Rapha, God our Healer. Forgiveness of our sins through the blood of Jesus Christ is God's first act of healing in our lives. God's mercy to us through the sacrifice of His Son triumphs over the just judgment we deserve. Salvation restores relationship with God and gives us access to His unlimited healing power. When we intentionally, thoughtfully, and prayerfully daily align our spirit, soul, and body with the truths in Scripture, we appropriate what Jesus died to give us and God's healing flows into us.

Summary

This foundational truth of forgiveness cannot be overstated. It is the "ground zero" of not only our relationship with God, ourselves, and others, but also the fountain through which abundant life flows. This abundant life is partly summed up in 3 John 2, *"Beloved, I pray that in all things [of life, my note] you may prosper and be in health, even as your soul prospers."* As our soul (mind, will, and emotions) is set free from the emotional debt of unforgiveness, all things, including our health, can prosper.

Chapter Two

Forgiveness Unpacked

"Forgiveness is the giving, and so the receiving, of life." George MacDonald

The most frequent form of the word forgiveness in the New Testament is *aphiemi*. It is an intense form of the word meaning to send: to send forth, send away, letting go as if the sins had never been committed. Forgiveness, then, is forcefully sending away sins so that, within us, it is as if they had never been committed This applies to our own sins committed or the sins of others against us.

To effectively live in the fullness of forgiveness, received and given, the first issue needing to be settled within ourselves is that at salvation, God has made peace with us through Jesus. God is not mad at us!!! When Jesus died on the Cross, He took all past, present, and future sins you and

I have committed or may commit. He also took all the past, present, and future sins of the one who has offended us. He died ONCE for them ALL! The inability to fully grasp this truth keeps a consciousness of sin alive within us, either consciousness of our own sins or the sins of others toward us. If that sin consciousness is alive within us then we cannot fully grasp or walk in what Jesus did for us. The old must entirely be released before totally receiving and walking in the new is possible.

The next place of confusion needing clarification is a Scripture we all can quote, Matthew 6:12-15. *"Forgive us our debts, as we also have forgiven our debtors...For if you forgive others for their transgressions, your heavenly Father will also forgive you. But if you do not forgive others, then your Father will not forgive your transgressions."*

Many people believe this passage is talking about their salvation--that if they do not forgive themselves or others--then they are not saved. However, this cannot be true because if Jesus died once for all our sins at one point in time, and we have accepted Him as our Savior, then sin is forgiven, past, present, and future. Looking at the whole word of God, 1Peter 3:18 and Colossians 2:13 confirm this truth. 1Peter 3:18 says, *"For Christ has suffered ONCE for sins..."* (emphasis mine). Colossians 2:13 says, *"When you were dead in your transgressions and the uncircumcision of your flesh, He made you alive together with Him, having forgiven us ALL our transgressions."* (Emphasis mine.)

So, if Matthew 6:12-15 is not about having or losing our salvation in Christ, what does it mean? It means that anything we want the grace to receive, we must seek the grace to give away. You cannot fill something that is already full. So, if we do not develop the capacity to fully forgive others--sending away and breaking the emotional connection to the offense--then we cannot fully receive and feel God's forgiveness of us. Galatians 6:7 is clear, we reap what we sow. The converse is also true, we cannot reap what we do not sow.

Forgiveness seems illogical and foolish to the natural mind. The natural mind and man want revenge, to give as good as they got, to mete out justice that they deem "fits the crime." The problem is we have never gotten the justice we deserve because of the blood of Jesus Christ, so who are we to impose justice on anyone? James 4:12 says that there is only one Lawgiver and Judge, God, so when we "mete out justice" we are taking God's place. When we set ourselves up as arbiter and judge, then we place ourselves between God and the other person, limiting what God can do in both parties.

Forgiveness Is Not....

There are many misunderstandings and misconceptions regarding forgiveness. These misconceptions become

11

hindrances to walking in the fullness of forgiveness. Some of the false beliefs are that forgiveness means to overlook an offense, being "OK" with it, pretending it never occurred, that you must forgive and forget, trusting the offender right away, or believing the offending party will go free. Overlooking an offense, being "OK" with it, or pretending it never happened are forms of denial. It is saying that the offense did not hurt.

By definition an offense is an action (or words) which insult, causing hurt or displeasure. It can be aggressive in nature, but not always. By saying something which causes insult, hurt or displeasure is OK and that it has been overlooked means it is "stuffed" within the spirit, soul and body of the person and not really addressed or resolved. Over time, this equates to a garbage compactor where the garbage keeps getting compacted, but never removed from the machine. After a while, it begins to leak and stink, and eventually affects the functioning of the machine. So it is with us. Never resolving the emotional debt that comes with offenses causes us to "leak and stink" into not only our relationship with others, but also with God and ourselves.

Many people also equate forgiveness with trust, which are two entirely different things. Forgiveness has to do with the past part of a relationship, where the offense occurred. Trust has to do with the future relationship and what might be built in the relationship going forward. When the differences between forgiveness and trust are unclear or muddied, often the offended party thinks that you must continue to like the person and/or be their friend. With this mindset, the offended person often sets themselves up for more heartbreak because the offender is not a safe person.

People confronted with their sin against others tend to be in denial (**D**.on't **E**.ven k**N**.ow **I**. **A**.m **L**.ying), defensive, thus self-protecting. If they eventually see the wound they have caused, they may say sorry, but want the issue to be over. They then pressure the other to have a fully restored, trusting relationship right away. However, in Matthew 3:8, John the Baptist gives a command for those who are offenders, "Produce fruit in keeping with repentance." Repentance is a complete, 180 degree, change in both mindset AND behavior. The offended party can wait to see if there is true repentance by a consistent change of behavior. Then trust will be rebuilt so that relationship can be fully restored. Here is an important axiom to remember: Forgiveness is given; trust is earned.

In addition, people cling to unforgiveness thinking it will protect them, giving them power over the offender. This mindset is a combination of the sin of vengeance and self-pity with which to deny the dysfunction in their lives. Seeking revenge is trying to do God's job for Him--which never works well for us. Vengeance belongs only to God. Romans 12:19. Self-pity is both deceptive and destructive because we see ourselves as victims. The victim mindset and mentality is contrary to the truth that as believers we are overcomers.

Sadly, holding offenses only punishes the one doing the holding. The anger, resentment, hatred, and judgment held onto has been said to be like drinking poison, waiting for the other person to die. Bitterness, a hard heart, and a mind and/or body that pays the price is the result. Further, Hebrews 12:15 is quite clear that when we allow bitterness to set into our spirit and soul through unforgiveness, not only does it affect us but also those around us. Few people stay very long in the company of a bitter person.

Summary

Forgiveness is an act of love both to ourselves and to others. It is an intense sending forth of the thoughts, feelings, and emotions resulting from an offense committed by someone toward us or towards ourselves. Forgiveness is not saying an offense is OK or overlooked when it is not. Forgiveness also is not the same as trust. Forgiveness is given, as God did for us through the blood of Jesus, trust is earned by the other person demonstrating repentance by bearing the fruit of change. Unforgiveness, the holding of offenses, does not protect us or punish the other person. It only isolates us from relationship with others, with a root of bitterness and judgment springing up, sowing seeds in our own lives that will be reaped.

Chapter Three

The Price of Not Forgiving

"As long as you don't forgive, who and whatever it is
will occupy a rent-free space in your mind."
Isabelle Holland

The price of holding unforgivenss is costly - spiritually, mentally, emotionally, and physically. When life is riddled with relationships where forgiveness has not fully been resolved, the effects begin to reveal themselves in many different ways. Patterns of brokenness in relationships begin to emerge. There can be mental/emotional patterns of depression, panic attacks, sleeplessness, etc. It is also possible that certain disease processes surface due to unresolved forgiveness issues. The pain can only be sustained for so long before our system begins to break down.

Spiritually

One of the biggest costs of unforgiveness is our

17

closeness and intimacy with God. When there is bitterness, our heart is not fully open to hear or receive what is flowing from Heaven. God is always speaking to us, indeed, His Word says His thoughts toward us are more than the sands of the seashore. Psalm 139:17-18. When we allow our hearts to be hardened by unforgiveness, bitterness, anger, resentment or even hatred, we can miss much of God's communication with us. When focused on an offense and the negative emotions creating turmoil in us, the offense is at the forefront of our eyes and heart, thus clouding and obstructing our ability to hear what God is saying to us.

Unforgiveness and bitterness weakens and distorts our relationship to God. Our thinking gets twisted and we may start to blame God for the way life now is. We also become more susceptible to believing the enemy's lies about the truth of Who God is and what He has provided for us through the death, burial, and resurrection of His Son. Not only that but we more fully align ourselves with the lies the enemy tells us about ourselves and others. Once we believe the lies of the enemy, very soon life gets off track, mired in the mindset of a victim rather than an overcomer.

On the Cross, Jesus demonstrated and modeled the example of how to be an overcomer in the face of injustice and unbelievable cruelty. He chose not to be a victim but rather trusted His Father even while feeling the one instance of isolation from Him. He chose forgiveness, to send away the offenses, along with the thoughts, feelings and emotions. In doing so, through His example, Jesus secured the victory for us as we do the same--maintaining heart connection not only with Father God but with others in the midst of difficult times.

There is another danger of allowing an offense to take root because of how it distorts our relationship to God. The offense can become an idol in our lives. Aiko Hormann[1] defines idolatry as "an undue attachment or **preoccupation** [emphasis mine] with persons [can be animals], things, or conditions...where one dwells, focuses, then gives power to."

It is well known that we can idolize another person, our pets and things like careers, money, sports, shopping, collections, health and fitness, etc. Enjoying any of these things is not wrong in and of themselves, but it is the attitude behind those things which make them idolatrous.

What is less understood is that we can set up an idol in our hearts by focusing on conditions in our souls like jealousy, worry, grief, anxiety, betrayal, fear, greed, rejection, resentment, bitterness, anger, happiness, and love, to

---

[1] Hormann, Aiko, Overcomer's Teacher's Manual (Self-published) pp. 151-153

name just a few. When we have undue focus on something, we give it power and it begins to take a more important place in our lives than God.

God hates idolatry in us and He will not tolerate it. Look at Ezekiel 14:3-5. *"Son of man, these men have set up their idols in their hearts and have put right before their faces the stumbling block of their iniquity. Should I be consulted by them at all? Therefore speak to them and tell them, 'Thus says the LORD God, "Any man of the house of Israel who sets up his idols in his heart, puts right before his face the stumbling block of his iniquity, and then comes to the prophet, I the LORD will be brought to give him an answer in the matter in view of the multitude of his idols, in order to lay hold of the hearts of the house of Israel who are estranged from Me through all their idols."'"*

An offense which is nursed and rehearsed becomes an idol. It becomes a stumbling block to our walk with Christ. Iniquity is a twisting or turning, not living aligned with truth, so the condition of our soul bonded to the offense, twists and turns our life away from God. He never forces us to do anything and lets us have our idol as long as we want it. He answers us according to those idols (allowing more of the same in our lives), longing and waiting for us to see the destruction they are exacting, waiting for us to finally hate the condition of our life so much that our hearts fully return to Him. God is waiting with open arms for just that moment because of His desire for intimate relationship with His children.

Is your relationship with God dry or silent? There can be many reasons. One of the first questions to ask Him and ourselves is if there is any unforgiveness or bitterness and judgments in our hearts. Ask Him if idols have been created by being bonded to an offense that is unresolved. Humbling ourselves to hear the answer and praying through the issue, whatever it takes, is a major step in restoring our intimacy with God. It also restores the blessing in our life and puts us on the path to more fully pursue the destiny God has for us.

Relationally

Not only is our relationship with God affected when we hold unforgiveness, but relationships with others begin to change as well. We know God created us for relationship--primarily with Him, but certainly others as well. When wounded by others we feel rejected and abandoned, which is the most painful experience humans can have. The human tendency is then to withdraw from relationship since it is painful to sustain. Holding on to offenses and unforgiveness isolates us from the very thing that is to give us life, when learning to walk fully in forgiveness provides the ability to maintain connection with others.

Judgment

One of the major effects of unforgiveness is in the area of bitter root judgment. Not understanding this principle not only keeps us tied to offenders and offenses, but brings destruction to our lives in other ways.

When teaching this principle I often start by asking, "Who has ever said to themselves, I will never be like my mother and/or father, but you open your mouth and out they come?" Without fail the audience twitters and sheepish looks roll over their faces. I then ask, "How many of you find yourselves in situations that are similar to ones you had growing up and you feel stuck in the pattern, like the movie Groundhog Day?" Again, the twitters and sheepish looks.

Years ago, a man came to our church in Alabama. He was a painter who was looking for work. Since we were moving in a few months, we asked him to paint the outside of our house, preparing it for sale. It was a hot and steamy Alabama summer, so the children and I would take him water or lemonade to make sure he was hydrated. Once when I took out some water he asked if he could speak to me. He said he knew I did prayer counseling at the church and he wanted some insight on a relationship situation. He blurted out that his wife had recently had an affair. He was heartbroken, sobbing, that he loved her and could not understand how she could do that to him, their marriage and family.

Prompted by the Holy Spirit I asked, "Who of your mother or father had an affair on the other one?"

His eyes got so big, they nearly fell out of his head. Stunned, he replied, "How did you know that? It was my mother."

A client of mine grew up in a household with a father who was both an alcoholic and a womanizer. To say the least, her life was chaotic growing up. Wanting to leave home as soon as possible to get some peace, she married right out of high school. On their first anniversary, she found her husband in bed with her best friend. She got a divorce and later married again. When she came to see me, her current husband was getting drunk every night of the week. She was living another nightmare from her childhood, devastated that the very thing she tried to be free from was again haunting her life.

In each instance, there was opportunity to explain how the principle of bitter root judgment is tied to both unforgiveness and idolatry and how it operates in our lives. It is one of the most intense driving forces behind destructive patterns imprisoning us. Understanding this principle and its effects on our life can bring tremendous revelation.

When we walk through the steps to bring healing, personal freedom and the potential for restored relationships is the result.

Hebrews 12:14-15 states, *"Strive to live in peace with everybody and pursue that consecration and holiness without which no one will [ever] see the Lord. Exercise foresight and be on the watch to look [after one another], to see that no one falls back from and fails to secure God's grace (His unmerited favor and spiritual blessing), in order that no root of resentment (rancor, bitterness, or hatred) shoot forth and causes trouble and bitter torment, and the many become contaminated and defiled by it."* Amplified Bible.

The book of Hebrews is written to believers in Christ. Therefore, from the Word, as believers we can allow a root of bitterness to spring up in our hearts when unforgiveness has lodged there too long. Unforgiveness plants seeds in our life, which when the right conditions occur, will be reaped as a crop of devastation. What we sow, we reap. Galatians 6:7. Those seeds may have been planted as a child and forgotten, especially when the family has not taught the children how to forgive, be angry yet not sin, discuss their problems, or how to take those hurts to Jesus for comfort and resolution. That is why it is critically important to daily bring hurts and wounds to Jesus, not only from the day, but to also ask Him to examine your heart for buried unresolved issues from the past.

The crops personally produced are increased isolation from people to prevent further hurt, a developing negative view of life where you see yourself as a victim instead of an overcomer, as well as potential health problems which will be discussed in the next section. Living this way is definitely not living in the fullness of God's grace on a daily basis--the abundant life Jesus died to give us.

Hebrews 12:15 shows us that not only are we affected personally by the unforgiveness seeds planted in our lives, but the bitterness coming from that crop defiles others around us. Defilement means to make filthy or dirty, to pollute, to make ceremonially unclean, to profane or sully. Literally our bitterness "slimes" others and some very discouraging, destructive patterns can begin to happen.

Another aspect to this is found in Matthew 7:1-2. *"Do not judge so that you will not be judged. For in the same way you judge, you will be judged; and by your standard of measure, it will be measured to you."* Romans 2:1 explains yet another facet of this issue. *"Therefore you have no excuse, every one of you who passes judgment, for in that which you judge another, you condemn yourself; for you who judge practice the same things."*

Because we are hurt, angry and bitter, we judge. However, Matthew 7:1-2 is clear. As we judge others, the same measure will come back to us. Others will then judge us in the same area of life. We begin to draw people to us repeatedly who treat us the same way. It is defilement at work.

Added to that is the admonition from Romans 2:1 which says that when you judge from a heart of bitterness, you are condemning yourself (defiling yourself) to practice the very things you judged. Not only do others repeatedly treat you according to your judgments, but also the bitter root judgments personally affect the way you behave towards others. Hence the twitters and sheepish looks from people when asked the questions about acting like their mother or father when they promised themselves they would never do those things.

Unrighteous judgment, based on unforgiveness with the bitter roots, brings a "double whammy" of harvest into our lives. Hosea 8:7 comes to mind. *"For they sow the wind and they shall reap the whirlwind. The standing grain has no heads; it shall yield no meal; if were to yield, strangers and aliens would eat it up."* Even if our lives produce fruit, the whirlwind of destruction blows the fruit away for others to "eat up."

Perhaps now the example of the house painter and my client make more sense. The painter had judged his mother for her affair which cost him a broken home and a chaotic childhood, being shuffled from parent to parent while having to listen to the bitterness coming from each of them. What he judged in his mother defiled his wife, who had also grown up in a family where the mother had had an affair. He picked a spouse who would fulfill what was buried but very active in his heart.

My client judged her father for his alcoholism and womanizing and the dysfunction it caused in her family. Now you can see why she chose the womanizer for her first husband and the alcoholic for her second. The unforgiveness in her heart which was never resolved planted seeds resulting in bitterness and judgment defiling not only herself but the men she chose, repeating patterns in her life (the crop that was reaped) she desperately tried to escape.

Let me clarify one point. Just because we defile others with our unforgiveness, bitterness, and judgment does not take away the free will of the other person to do what is righteous in each situation. We are all responsible for the choices we make. However, the places in us that are defiled by others are generally weak places of which we are unaware. They may have occurred in childhood and were buried or they could be ones we have refused to look at (stronghold of denial) because of the pain involved. One

27

other possibility is that we believe we have taken care of the problem by forgiving the offending party. However, ignorance of how we have sinned in painful situations by allowing bitterness, judgment, and defilement to work together in us keeps the issue alive in our lives, bearing bitter fruit until we repent and take our sin to the Cross.

Both the painter and my client pursued healing for their pain. The painter and his wife sought marriage counseling and after some months were able to save their marriage, both having worked on their individual places of unforgiveness, bitterness and judgment. My client returned three weeks after that first session with an amazing story. From her simple act of genuine repentance for her unforgiveness, bitterness, and judgment toward her father, for sending away the thoughts, feelings, and emotions buried in her heart, for asking Jesus to cleanse her unsaved husband from the defilement of her sins, he immediately quit drinking during the week and only had a small amount on the weekends. Since her husband did not know she was coming for ministry, her act of resolving her sinful responses to childhood traumas resulted in freedom for both she and her husband, putting them on the path to a restored relationship.

Vows and Self-Covenants

One other thing usually happens when bitterness

28

and judgment have set in. We often make declarations to ourselves or others regarding the offense. We say things like, "I will never... or I will always..." These declarations are a self-promise, a vow or a covenant we make with ourselves. Those declarations then become something in our lives that must be fulfilled. Proverbs 18:21 says, *"Death and life are in the power of the tongue, those who love it, will eat its fruit."*

These declarations have great influence because they are tied to bitterness and judgment. Some of them even sound righteous like, "I will never hit women." At face value that certainly sounds like a good thing. However, that statement alone exposes a lie it is easy for the enemy to get us to believe. When said, we are declaring that WE will make it happen. It is like putting yourself under a law, binding yourself to fulfill that very thing in your own strength. It does not recognize God or call on Him to help us transform our hearts and character to walk out righteous behavior.

Vows and self-covenants can be so powerful that can also affect our physiology. A woman client was distressed because she was unable to sustain a pregnancy. The couple had one child but that birth had been followed by repeated miscarriages. While praying for her, the Lord gave me a word of knowledge that she had been molested as a child. Asking her about that, she told me she had been molested by her grandfather. We prayed through prayers of forgiveness and judgment. Next the Lord impressed upon me to ask her if she had ever made some kind of vow about the situation. Immediately she remembered what she had spoken over herself frequently while the molestation was continuing, "If this is what being a child is like, I never want to have children of my own." Her body was responding to the vow she had made. We took that vow to the Cross and broke the curse of it over her life. Within six weeks she was pregnant and delivered twins nine months later. The couple also went on to have additional children and there were no further miscarriages!

Her life and the life of her husband had paid a price, "eating the fruit of her lips." Our lives are no different. Vows and self-covenants made from unforgiveness and bitterness truly can have that much power. Often they have been made and forgotten but unconscious and still profoundly affecting us in the spiritual, mental, emotional, and physiological areas of life.

Physiologically

There are significant physiological consequences to broken or nonexistent relationship. In the extreme, the cost of non-relationship became known after World War II, in both United States and Romanian orphanages. Thirty-seven percent of babies who were separated from their

mothers for whatever reason, given basic care in an or-
phanage but little if any interaction with others, would first
withdraw into themselves by not responding to caregivers
and eventually die. The others began to exhibit forms of
mental illness.[2]

Less extreme, but nevertheless costly, physiological
consequences occur when unforgiveness, bitterness and
judgment are not fully resolved by sending away (*aphiemi*)
the offense to the Cross. The soul connection to the
thoughts, feelings and emotions attached to the offense
must also be sent away.

Every experience you have ever had since concep-
tion is recorded within you as a memory. The memories
within us are mental and emotional and of course, have a
spiritual component as well. Rather than being stored solely
in the brain as was believed, Candace Pert[3] made a remark-
able discovery about 20 years ago. She found that emotions
are stored all over the body as "chemical packets."

All the memories we have ever had are stored in us
with an emotional "chemical packet" attached to them.
When that memory is triggered by thinking about it or be-

---

[2] Szalavitz, Maia and Perry, Bruce D. M.D., PhD, Born For
Love, (New York, NY, Harper Collins, 2010) pp. 50-55.
[3] Pert, Candace The Molecules of Emotion (New York, NY: Si-
mon and Schuster, 1999)

ing reminded of it in some way, then that chemical packet is released and we experience the same emotions we did as when the first event occurred. Even if it is not triggered, the memory is still stored with the chemical packet attached. Those packets are affecting us because what is stored within them is either stress chemicals or "peace" chemicals.

Stress is a familiar term to us. Talk to someone for a short time and often you will hear that they are stressed either by their words or by the emotion in their voices. Stress can be good when we are getting away from some form of danger, but prolonged stress has been proven to be detrimental to well-being in every area of life.

Without getting too technical, our body is designed to live in chemical balance. There really is too much of a good thing. People can die from drinking too much water at one time and it is possible to poison yourself by eating too many carbohydrates (sugars) at one time. Just like water and the carbohydrates that come from fruits and vegetables are good for us, the stress hormones of adrenaline and cortisol serve important functions in the body. Needing to get out of the way of a speeding train or rescue a child from an oncoming car, stress hormones are quickly released to give the extra energy and stamina needed to resolve the crisis.

When the crisis is over, if there are no other forms of crisis or experiences of anger or frustration, the body recovers its chemical balance in 72 hours. However, continual stress, therefore a continual release of these hormones in the body keep it revved up and in a state of alert. When we are in conflict within ourselves or with others, there is a level of unhealthy stress, keeping our bodies revved up on adrenaline and cortisol.

When the body cannot come back into balance, cortisol is especially harmful. It has been said that too much cortisol for too long literally eats up the body from the inside out. The human body can be in either a state of growth or survival, not both simultaneously. One of the effects of too much cortisol is that it erases newly made connections in the brain leading to growth. This is why people under severe stress often say their memory is "going." New areas of memory are literally dissolved until the stress is resolved and the body shifts back into growth mode. Excessive cortisol from stress also tells the body to store fat in the abdomen. The medical community has made a strong correlation between abdominal fat and heart disease. Finally, prolonged cortisol release begins to affect all other organ systems in the body, first with exhaustion, then with failure.

Areas of unforgiveness in our lives are constructed of memories with the stress chemical packets attached. Thus, we have an emotional connection to an offense, and until the connection is severed, it is still affecting us negatively, controlling us to some degree, and affecting our health because of the stress chemicals attached to it.

When something is extremely hurtful we tend to replay it over and over in our minds, like being in a hamster wheel. As the memories are triggered by seeing the person, someone talking about the person or incident, or we just nurse and rehearse the incident, the stress chemicals are released. Every time we think about an incident which hasn't been fully forgiven, our body reacts the same way it did when the offense occurred. More of the stress chemicals are released and they flood our body with the resulting detrimental effects.

What if you are the kind of person who is able to stuff things, who, like Scarlett O'Hara in <u>Gone With the Wind</u>, lives by the credo, "I'll think about it tomorrow." Just as with Scarlett, however, tomorrow never comes. Observation of many people over the years has shown me how this works. They come for ministry and will be talking about an event in their lives. Emotion will begin to rise up as evidenced by eyes swelling with tears, restlessness, or taking deep breaths. Then just as suddenly, it gets hidden. It has been swallowed, stuffed somewhere deep within. It can be a conscious or unconscious thing that happens. Their countenance is again serene and peaceful, but is it gone or resolved, no longer affecting the person or those in his or her life? Hardly.

Some recent some recent studies in medical research and the science of quantum physics give us a new picture of the heart and how the human body functions at the subatomic level. (Quantum physics is the study of the smallest amount of a physical quality that can exist independently. It is especially described as the smallest amount of electromagnetic radiation.) Understanding these discoveries and some rudimentary basics of quantum physics shows the harmony of science and Biblical principles. This provides insights which should motivate us to quickly resolve offenses and to forgive as enlightened self-interest. By loving and forgiving ourselves as well as loving others as we love ourselves (Matthew 22:39), we are, in fact, choosing life. Holding on to unforgiveness, bitterness, judgment and offenses is really a form of self-hatred. Let me show you why.

Quantum physics has revealed the truth that every form of matter vibrates and has a frequency. Machines which can measure the vibrational frequencies of matter have long been used in industry. Medical research is now using machines such as these for various diagnostic and treatment purposes.

The HeartMath Institute[4] uses these machines to measure the electromagnetic vibrations which emanate

---

[4] For more information and resources visit www.heartmath.com.

from a person's heart. They discovered that our hearts give off an electromagnetic field (vibration) which can be measured up to 12 feet from the body. The brain also gives off a field, but it can only be measured 2-3 feet from the body. The heart, then, is a 5000 times more powerful electromagnetic generator than the brain.

What spurred interest in this area of study were the incredible stories surfacing from the recipients of heart transplants. For instance, a middle aged man who received a heart from a teenage boy woke up and enjoyed heavy metal rock music, when, before surgery, he abhorred it. Another man woke up and told his wife everything was "copacetic," when he had never used the word before. Doing some investigation, it was found that the heart donor and his wife would use copacetic when they made up after a fight. The most amazing story, however, was of a young girl who received the heart of another young girl who had been murdered. The heart recipient began having nightmares about being stabbed in such vivid detail that they were able to apprehend the perpetrator who had indeed murdered the heart donor by stabbing.

One of the first discoveries was that 60-65% of the heart is neural cells--the same cells as in the brain, using the same chemicals and links. The "heart brain" is in continual communication with the emotion centers of the "head brain." Because the "heart brain" stores memories, it directs the "head brain" to make "appropriate" emotional responses to current situations from what is stored there. Think about it, the heart is the only organ in your body which, with every beat, affects every cell in your body on a continual basis at the same time.

The heart is now classified as part of the hormonal system because it produces and secretes hormones to regulate stress and promote love and social bonding. Every heartbeat literally signals the brain for either stress (fear) or peace. Every heartbeat signaling stress or peace affects the "switches" on our DNA, which tell the body how to function. Because the heart is more powerful than the brain, whatever beliefs are in the heart will always trump what is in the mind. Therefore life will always be lived out with what is in the heart, whether buried or conscious.

Feelings buried alive never die! This is often the motivation behind why we do the things we don't want to do. Out of sight may be out of the conscious mind, but not out of the soul. Neither denial nor avoidance sends away offenses or breaks the emotional connection to them.

Since the heart is now known to have a "brain" and store memory, science now supports the Bible, rather than conflicting with it. Proverbs 4:23 comes to mind, *"Watch over your heart with all diligence, For from it flow the springs [issues, KJV] of life."* Matthew 18:35 is clear that for-

37

giveness is a heart issue *"This is how my heavenly Father will treat each of you unless you forgive your brother from your HEART,"* [emphasis mine].

The discoveries regarding the heart were astonishing to the medical community. However, quantum physics research has taken understanding of the human body to an even deeper level. It shows how the matter in the body works at the subatomic level. Each organ and organ system in our body vibrates at a certain healthy frequency. When our body is in a state of peace rather than stress, those frequencies harmonize with each other. Where there are stress chemical packets attached to memories, the vibrations coming from them are not healthy because they are not harmonizing with love [peace]. They create dissonance and disharmony wherever they are stored in the body. Letting the sun go down on your anger (Ephesians 4:26), sleeping on it, causes the negative frequencies to be buried in your body. The longer they remain, the more effect they have on the tissue surrounding them, causing damage. The disharmonious frequencies begin to weaken and set up "dis-ease" in the organ and organ system, eventually affecting the whole body.

When there is true, full forgiveness, the negative, disharmonious chemical packets and frequencies are changed to positive (energy never goes away, it only changes form). The body then begins to release the hormones serotonin and DHEA, which are twenty times more soothing than morphine or heroin and stronger than any other drug. Your spirit, soul and body can heal itself because the dissonance has changed to harmony and the release of serotonin and DHEA begins to restore emotional health.

Not forgiving from the heart by forcefully sending away not only the offense but also breaking the emotional connection to the thoughts, words, and emotions attached to the offense keeps the negative emotional packet affecting your spirit, soul, and body in harmful ways. Not releasing it, choosing to hold onto it is like punishing yourself for what someone else did to you or what you might have done to yourself. Because Jesus paid for all sin (yours included) for all time at the Cross, why wouldn't you give it up? Not to, then, is that act of self-hatred.

Summary

Holding on to offenses, refusing to give them up, creates bitterness and bitter root judgments. There is now a layer of our own sin to be taken to the Cross. It is no longer just about the person offending us. Seeds of bitterness and judgment planted in our hearts will grow a crop which will be reaped through repeated patterns of the same type of wounding or we will act like the very person or thing we have judged. Usually, both happens.

There are very real costs to unforgiveness, spiritually, relationally, and physically. Spiritually, we lose our intimate connection with God because we are bowing to the idols of unforgiveness and bitterness. Relationally, we isolate ourselves by building walls in our hearts, allowing them to become hardened and stony. Relationships suffer and the very thing for which we were created becomes a source of pain to be avoided. Physiologically our bodies pay a price for holding onto the stress created by unforgiveness. The "dis-ease" in our spirits and souls sets up the potential for and eventually creates disease in our bodies.

Chapter Four

Reconciling Emotional Debt

"When you hold resentment toward another, you are bound to that person or condition by an emotional link that is stronger than steel. Forgiveness is the only way to dissolve that link and get free." Catherine Ponder

God has given us the way to resolve emotional debt if we choose it. There is a cost in our lives to walking in forgiveness, just as there was for Jesus. It is death to the kingdom of self. (What I want, when I want it, how I want it--and don't get in my way.) The irony is that when we die to self, we get more life, the life of Christ in us. Because Jesus, on the Cross, forgave, when we truly walk out forgiveness from our hearts, we are allowing the life of Christ to flow through us, showing others the way. We become a walking letter of Christ, a testimony,

41

not a sermon. People yearn to see life that works and are drawn to ask why it is so.

Before looking at the process, the "how to" of forgiveness, let me address some roadblocks which may occur along the way. Several of these have been discussed in the section of "What Forgiveness is Not," and you can review them there. However, there are a few distinct other snares of which to be aware.

Hindrances

1. JUDGMENT.

Even though this has been addressed, it cannot be overemphasized. My experience in two plus decades of ministry is that very few people have heard nor do they understand that forgiveness is not complete until your sins of judgment, bitterness and the resulting vows have been repented for and given to Jesus. There is no realization of their own sin as a result of the offense toward them. They have no concept of the seeds of bitterness, judgment, and vows sown which will be reaped in repeated destructive patterns in their lives. No wonder people feel stuck and cannot be free to move in the destiny God has for them.

2. FORGIVING OURSELVES.

Many times the hardest thing we must do is forgive ourselves. We have all made foolish, immature choices at times. That is an inescapable fact. Sometimes we have done awful things. When we go to God and are truly repentant for what we have done, we are immediately forgiven. God drops our sins into the depths of the sea. Micah 7:19. Our slate is wiped clean.

Why keep yourself in prison and hostage to unforgiveness, bitterness, judgment and vows? You cannot pay for your own sin. Refusal to forgive yourself is saying that the blood of Jesus is not enough and couldn't possibly have paid for THAT sin! It is a form of idolatry, since we are bonded to a condition within ourselves, not appropriating and living out what Jesus died on the Cross to give us.

Forgiving ourselves does not mean we are free of the consequences of our choices. True repentance always bears fruit, the fruit of repentance. That fruit is swallowing our pride, and, as far as humanly possible, confessing what has been done, repenting, disciplining ourselves to walk in new ways, and making restitution.

Restitution is the Old and New Testament principle of restoring what was broken, stolen, or lost and adding one-fifth to it. See Numbers 5:6-8; Luke 19:1-10. It is the consequence we walk out. Accepting and diligently following through with restitution without complaining demonstrates our hearts are sincerely devoted to restoring relationship and that we are willing to let God write the lesson on our hearts. It demonstrates bearing the fruit of repentance.

3. GUILT--TRUE AND FALSE.

Resolving guilt is a significant issue for an abundant life. When we have done something or think we have done something wrong, we experience guilt. It can be either true or false guilt. Guilt looks for who is responsible for the blame and who will meet the obligation to make good either through punishment or compensation. Guilt is the mind's way of saying, "This is not who you are." It creates dissonance (stress) within us and when not resolved there is a toll on our spirit, soul, and body.

True guilt means I have sinned. It is a gift God created within us to let us know when we have done wrong. It is meant to move us to take responsibility, admit we are to blame, and to make it right. True guilt is supposed to move us quickly to God and the offended one, repenting to both, and making restitution. The goal is restored relationship.

False guilt is feeling responsible for something that is not your sin. It is taking on guilt that rightfully belongs to another person. False guilt comes when we have unconsciously, emotionally "partnered" with another's sin or wrongdoing. It is a burden we are not to carry.

A woman came to see me. She was experiencing burnout from trying to make sure everything in her life was under control. When something got away from her, she was overwhelmed with anxiety and crushing guilt paralyzed her for days or weeks. As she related her story, God revealed where the root had been planted in her life.

Growing up, her divorced mother would leave her and her sister, ages 6 and 4, alone all night while she went out drinking. One night her younger sister fell and hurt herself while the mother was gone. When the mother came home, she berated the oldest child for letting her sibling get hurt. For years the mother heaped guilt upon that child, blaming her for not protecting her sister. This woman had carried the burden of false guilt for years. When Jesus showed her that she was holding a mountain of false guilt, she happily gave it to Him. Knowing the truth brought tremendous relief to her. As she continued to walk in the truth, bringing down the stronghold of false guilt, her anxiety abated. She was also able to release the need to control because she was now able to trust God to keep disasters at bay.

If there is guilt in your heart, ask Jesus to show you whether it is true or false. If true, then quickly repent, humble yourself and as much as possible, do what you can to make restitution. If false, then take it to the Cross and leave it there! Be aware, however, that hidden under that false guilt may be issues of unforgiveness toward whomever pushed it on you. You may have to forgive yourself for taking it on, even though you may have been too little to understand what was happening. Be sure to ask the Lord if there are judgments and vows which also need to go to the Cross.

4. SHAME.

Holding unforgiveness and guilt opens the doorway to shame. Shame is the heart's way of saying, "I reject you, you are fatally flawed." Shame brings self-condemnation with the expectation of judgment. Living in fear of judgment causes many self-protecting behaviors, all of which produce increased stress. When we live in shame we begin to engage in self-sabotaging behaviors so we can punish ourselves, creating more shame and more stress. It is a self-destruct cycle because we cannot shame ourselves into a healthy relationship with ourselves or others. It keeps us stuck at an emotionally immature level. Jesus already took the punishment for us, despising the shame, so we can live free of it.

Physiologically, there are effects as well. Our body goes into survival rather than growth mode because of the stress.

5. SATAN'S SCHEMES.

It would be remiss of me if I did not mention the enemy's schemes to thwart our walking in the freedom of forgiveness. He will do all he can to disrupt the process. He will bombard with every kind of temptation so that we will reopen the wound and never let it heal.

Why does he do that? Simple. We are created for relationship. The unity in healthy relationship in Christ terrifies him because of the power that results, thus the furthering of the Kingdom. Any way he can destroy relationship between God and man or man and man is his goal. The strategy is to keep us focused more on ourselves and our wounds than on God and being conduits of the Kingdom.

Summary

By not understanding the hindrances to full forgiveness, we remain unable to fully walk in freedom. Knowing how the judgment we sow into our lives keeps us in bondage is critical to totally resolving a situation. Equally important is comprehending how unforgiveness held toward others along with guilt and shame make a three-fold cord which keeps us oppressed and in bondage. Finally, we cannot be ignorant of the enemy's schemes to keep us bound, to destroy the very things for which we were created, relationship.

Chapter Five

The Process of Forgiving

"Inner peace can be reached only when we practice forgiveness." Gerald G. Jampolsky

Because forgiveness is foundational to our life in Christ, the need is to know how to practically engage it in our lives. What follows is a model, not a set of rules. Always be attuned to the Holy Spirit as you walk out the principles of forgiveness as He may change things. It is helpful, though, to have an outline to follow until the principles become habit in us.

When the choice is made to forcefully send away an offense (forgive), then the choice is to live in peace and be a peacemaker. True peace, *shalom,* in Hebrew, means nothing missing, nothing broken in any area of life. Until forgiveness is totally worked out in a situation, there can be no true peace within ourselves or in relationship to others.

The Model

1. Start with Prayer.
    a. Focus on your heart and God.
    b. Begin asking God to show you those whom you need to forgive. Write a list if necessary.

2. Verbalize forgiveness toward that person and for what they did.
    a. Release the person.
    b. Leave them and the offense at the cross.
3. Ask yourself these questions about the hurt and pain caused by the offense:
    a. What did Jesus do about this on the Cross?
    b. Am I willing to do anything about this?
    c. What will I do?
    d. When will I do it?
    e. Identify what you are feeling, what is coming from your heart.
    f. Give it a name--stress, anxiety, fear, anger, bitterness, shame, revenge, etc.
    i. Declare some affirmations:
        1. I don't want you (e.g., bitterness).
        2. I don't need you.
        3. You do not benefit my life.
        4. I send you away to the Cross.
        5. Ask Jesus to cut the emotional connection to the offense in your spirit, soul, and body.

6. Ask Jesus to show or tell you what He is doing with it.
7. Discern what you feel.
8. Repeat the process until you feel nothing but peace.

4. Ask God to show you where you may have made judgments.
   a. Repent for the judgments.
   b. Ask for the blood of Jesus to cleanse you.
   c. Ask for Him to bring the judgment(s) to death in you.
   d. Ask Jesus to destroy the harvest of the judgments in your life.
   e. Ask Him to cleanse others in your life from the defilements of your judgments.
   f. Ask for a restoration of relationship.

5. Ask God to show you if there are any vows attached to the judgments.
   a. Repent for them as specifically as you can.
   b. Ask for the blood of Jesus to cleanse your spirit, soul, and body from the vow(s) and bring them to death in your life.
   c. Affirm that the only covenant that you want in your life is the covenant you made with God, through Jesus Christ.

6. Ask God to show you the lies you have believed about God, yourself, or others because of this situation.

    a. Repent for believing the lies.
    b. Ask Jesus to cleanse the lies with His blood.
    c. Ask and immediately listen for truth to replace the lies.
    d. Ask for the truth to fill the places where the lies have lived.
    e. Affirm that you receive the truth.
    f. Choose to order your life according to the truth, even when the lie still seems like truth.

7. Ask God if there is anything you need to do to restore relationship or make restitution.

    a. Pray about God's timing to accomplish them. Do it when He tells you.
    b. Be a person of integrity and as far as humanly possible walk out the restoration and restitution without complaining, joyfully, allowing God to write any lessons needed on your heart.

8. Stand against the schemes of the enemy.

    a. Don't let the enemy tempt you into renewing the emotional connection to the offense by opening the gateway of your thoughts. Don't give any life to the situation.

b. Remind yourself that you have forgiven and will not be moved from that place.

c. On purpose, "Philippians 4:8" every thought which comes to you. Discipline your mind to think on the things that are true, honest, just, pure, lovely, of good report, things of virtue and praise.

    i. If the thoughts are relentless, speak out loud the things which meet the criteria of Philippians 4:8. Vocalizing the blessings you have received as a child of God is a good way to start. It has been proven that when vocalizing, you cannot think of other things.

    ii. Focusing on the forgiveness received through Christ's sacrifice for you will help move you toward gratitude, expressed by a similar willingness to forgive others.

d. Deliberately evoke the **emotion**, not just the thought of gratitude.

    i. The emotion of gratitude is the antidote to negative emotions. It cancels the negative vibrations and transforms them to positive, releasing the stress chemical packets and replacing that packet with peace chemicals. Those peace chemicals harmonize with the vibration of love.

Peace, then, allows you to receive God's love in greater measure, bringing healing to the spirit, soul, and body.

ii. The **emotion** of gratitude, more than anything else, quickly strengthens the brain's pathways to the "joy center" of the brain. The stronger the "joy center," the quicker the freedom of forgiveness is sustained.[5]

---

[5] The "joy center" is actually the right, pre-frontal orbital cortex in the brain. Neuro-biologically our entire identity is built on the capacity to experience joy and return to joy from distressing situations. Without this foundation of joy, our identity is based on lies, potentially crippling relationships throughout life.

It is supposed to be built in the first two years of life by mutual delight in relationship--being the sparkle in someone's eyes. As an infant, this is how love is perceived. The "joy center" is also strengthened by being helped to consistently return to joy (peace) from negative emotional states.

When sufficiently developed, the "joy center" regulates serotonin levels (the "feel good" neuro-transmitter), has executive control over the immune system, physical/emotional pain, and the entire emotional system including the primal drive centers of hunger, terror, rage, and sexual impulses. When well developed it is also larger and more powerful than the fear areas of the brain.

The brain is now described by medical science as having neuro-plasticity, meaning instead of being hard-wired and unable to adapt, the brain can change and grow. It is especially amazing to note, that the "joy center" retains the same physiological structure as a fetus. Therefore, the "joy center" is more easily reprogrammed with the result that if it was not well developed in the first two years of life, it can be strengthened later and be-

    iii.   My way of evoking the emotion of gratitude is to recall a memory of when God answered a prayer for me--and there was no doubt it was God. I focus on that memory and feel the wonder, the joy, and most of all the gratitude connected to that experience. My body is flooded with peace as I maintain that focus. In a very short amount of time, the negative emotion has gone and the enemy has been defeated.

  e. Ask the Holy Spirit to prompt you when you are in the old thought patterns that align with the lies of the enemy. Sometimes we have built a such a fortress and habit of thought surrounding the lie that we are unaware we have slipped back into old ways of thinking.

    i.   When prompted by the Holy Spirit, repent for slipping back into the old way.

    ii.   On purpose, re-engage walking in the precepts of Philippians 4:8 and stir up the emotion of gratitude to restore peace, strengthening your "joy center."

    iii.   Consistently doing this whenever the Holy Spirit prompts you results in in-

---

come more dominant than the primal brain centers. It then operates as it was designed--returning us to peace!

The joy of the Lord truly is our strength! Nehemiah 8:10.

creased periods of time where there is freedom. There will come a tipping point where the freedom will be sustained long term.

Summary

Working through the model can take some time initially but the effort results in freedom and the transformation of your life. Once you are familiar with the model it is easier. Learning to catch offenses immediately shortens the process considerably because bitterness and judgments have not had time to grow deep roots.

Making forgiveness the attitude and habit of life opens the doorway to intimacy with God, creativity in ourselves and relationships which reflect the nature of Heaven. Forgiveness *is* the gateway to healing, not just in our spirits and bodies, but it also brings peace to our souls. We are created for relationship and forgiveness is the healing power that makes them thrive.

COVENANT OF PEACE PRESENTATIONS:

For seminars, workshops, or speaking engagements,
contact Linda Forster at:

linda.forster68gmail.com
Or by phone: 717-648-4231

Books by Linda Forster

Loved to Life Manual –

A 16 lesson course on the basics of maturing in Christ. $25.00, plus $3.00 shipping and handling.

Forgiveness: Gateway to Healing –

$8.99, plus $3.00 shipping and handling.

Publications of Covenant of Peace Ministries,
linda.forster68gmail.com, 717-648-4231

Make checks payable to:

Covenant of Peace,
16 Gunpowder Road,
Mechanicsburg, PA 17050

40% Discount given for the purchase of 5 or more items.